Trees for
small gardens

D0300271

Cover: the lovely Prunus 'Shimidsu Sakura', one of the last of the Japanese cherries to bloom, in mid-May

Overleaf: the tupelo, Nyssa sylvatica, in the full glory of its autumn colour; although slow-growing, it can eventually become a large tree (both photographs by Michael Warren)

Trees for small gardens

A Wisley handbook
Keith Rushforth

Cassell

The Royal Horticultural Society

Cassell Educational Limited
Artillery House, Artillery Row
London SW1P 1RT
for the Royal Horticultural Society

First published 1987
Reprinted 1989

British Library Cataloguing in Publication Data

Rushforth, Keith
  Trees for small gardens.—New ed.—
  (A Wisley handbook).
  1. Ornamental trees
  I. Title II. Knight, F.P. III Royal Horticultural
Society IV. Series
  635.9'77   SB435

  ISBN 0–304–31108–1

Photographs by Michael Warren and Keith Rushforth
Design by Lesley Stewart

Phototypesetting by Chapterhouse Typesetting Ltd., Formby
Printed in Hong Kong by Wing King Tong Co. Ltd

Contents

Introduction

Trees are essential to any garden, contributing a beauty and a presence which no other plant or feature can provide. They fill a host of roles, giving scale and a framework to the surroundings, shade on hot summer afternoons, a colourful display of flower, fruit, foliage or bark. Trees are needed whatever the size and shape of the garden. However, small gardens demand extra care and thought in the use, choice and location of trees. The object of this book is to assist in the selection, planting, pruning and management, and simply the enjoyment, of trees in small gardens.

A dictionary definition of a tree is 'a perennial woody plant with an evident trunk', which is somewhat vague. The tallest tree in the world, a coastal redwood, *Sequoia sempervirens*, is as tall as the dome of St Paul's Cathedral at 364 ft (111 m), yet most trees are very much smaller. The term 'tree' is used here to include all woody plants which have, or can be trained to have, a single stem and will grow more than 13 ft (4 m) tall. Several very useful 'trees' for small gardens might be termed large shrubs in larger spaces.

A small garden may range in size from the back garden typical of new housing estates, only about 20 by 30 ft (6 by 9 m), to one measuring some 50 by 70 ft (15 by 21 m). Even in the smallest space, trees are necessary to bring out the best of the garden. In a larger area, the requirement is often not for larger trees, but for more trees, or for trees used to create a series of intimate rooms.

The tightly clustered, bright red berries of *Sorbus scalaris*, ripening in October, are set off by fronds of glossy leaves

The value of trees in a small garden

Choosing a tree just because you like it or its description may achieve a satisfactory result but is unlikely to maximize the potential of the garden. This chapter aims to give general guidance on the selection of trees for a small garden, taking account of their attributes, such as shape and scale, leaves and flowers, screening and support, and relating these to the overall scheme. (For detailed information on individual trees, see pp.34–58.)

SCALE

One of the beauties of a tree is that it is usually the largest object in the garden. However, a tree which is several times taller than everything else will often be totally out of proportion and, instead of enhancing a situation, may dominate it. It is important therefore to consider not just the physical size of the tree but its scale in relation to its surroundings and to other features of the garden.

Shape is equally relevant. A tall narrow shape can be used to punctuate a view or to lead the eye skywards and will be in keeping with high buildings. Examples range from the obelisks of certain very compactly upright or fastigiate forms, such as *Prunus* 'Amanogawa' and *Chamaecyparis lawsoniana* 'Columnaris', to more loosely upright trees like *Sorbus rehderiana* 'Joseph Rock'. A widespreading tree, however, will be more appropriate in a low and sprawling setting, although there are occasions when a discordant element can be useful, perhaps to accentuate the predominant features of the site. Among spreading trees with arching branches are *Sorbus scalaris* and *Acer davidii*. Those with a weeping habit, such as *Pyrus salicifolia* 'Pendula' and *Alnus incana* 'Pendula' can be used to form tumbling fountains of foliage.

A tree must also relate to space within the garden and should not be overbearing where this is limited, as in a small garden. A tree will generally be too large if it is taller or broader than the open space in front of it. As a rough guide, the tree should be from half to two thirds as tall and wide as the length and breadth of the entire garden. For instance, in a garden 33 ft (10 m) long and 20 ft (6 m) wide, a tree 16 to 23 ft (5–7 m) tall with a spread of around 13 ft (4 m) planted at one end should be in scale both with the space and with the lawn of 16 by 23 ft (5 by 7 m). However, trees which are either very narrow and tall or very broad and low can safely exceed this figure, so long as they are in harmony with other aspects of the site, without becoming too imposing.

SHADE

The shade of a tree can be welcome on a hot summer day and a nuisance at other times. All trees cast shade, which is an important factor to remember before planting them, and their shape and location should be considered in relation to the position of the sun and the times of day when the garden, or sun on the house, will be most appreciated. The density of shade, which is determined by the way the leaves fit together, should also be taken into account. Trees with small or pinnate leaves (where the leaf is composed of a number of small leaflets), like birch or rowan, cast light shade, while trees with large leaves, such as whitebeam, cast a heavier shade. However, this is not absolute and holly, which has small closely set leaves, casts a thick shade.

The density of shade will affect the use of the ground beneath. Deep shade may give a cool spot for sitting out in a hot summer but could be disastrous if you wish to grow plants there. Lighter, more dappled shade is needed for the purpose, provided by trees such as oak which are deep rooting and do not cause severe root competition with other plants. This sort of shade is particularly suitable for rhododendrons and other woodland plants. If shade is required over a patio or terrace, avoid trees like *Prunus*, *Acer* and *Tilia*, which are liable to become infested with aphids producing sticky honeydew. It is also wise to choose trees which are in full leaf by the beginning of May – in the British climate the one hot day of the year is just as likely to be then as in August!

FOLIAGE, FLOWERS, FRUIT AND BARK

Apart from being attractive in themselves, the foliage, flowers, fruit or bark of a tree will influence its appearance within the garden and in turn alter the perceived scale. For instance, large leaves, flowers or fruits tend to be more visible and thus make a space seem smaller. They are useful for achieving an effect of enclosed intimacy or for shortening a long vista, perhaps in a narrow garden, but can be claustrophobic in a pocket-sized plot. Here, trees with small leaves, flowers or fruits, or large leaves composed of many small leaflets, can be recommended, to emphasize space and make the small seem bigger. To take two examples from a single genus, *Sorbus* – *S. thibetica* 'John Mitchell' with its large simple leaves will create a feeling of smallness and closeness, whereas the feathery foliage of S. *vilmorinii*, with many small leaflets, will give the illusion of distance and expansiveness.

Leaves. The leaves are the most numerous and prominent components of a tree. Their green colour is due to chlorophyll, which converts the energy in sunlight to manufacture sugars, and there are usually other pigments present which can also absorb sunlight to carry out photosynthesis. When these are plentiful, as in many forms of the popular Japanese maple, *Acer palmatum*, they lead to purple, red, gold, or yellow foliage. The proportions of the two groups of compounds may change as the foliage matures, so the leaves emerge in one colour and take on a different hue later. For instance, *Aesculus neglecta* 'Erythroblastos' has pink young leaves which turn pale green and the bluish green foliage of *Pinus sylvestris* 'Aurea' becomes light gold in winter.

Leaves may also have a silvery or grey appearance, caused by hairs reflecting the light, as in *Pyrus salicifolia* 'Pendula', or by a waxy covering which prevents water loss, as in conifers like *Abies koreana*.

Variegated leaves, in which two or more colours are mixed together – frequently white or cream with green – are usually the result of some physiological oddity in the plant. Many variegated plants revert and produce shoots with plain green leaves, which must be removed in order to maintain the effect.

Leaves are deciduous, if they are lost each year in the autumn; or evergreen, in which case they are lost at various times of the year, so that the tree is never leafless; or semi-evergreen, when they are normally evergreen and lost only in severe winters or just before the new leaves grow. Many deciduous plants display bold and attractive autumn colours on the dying leaves.

Flowers. Compared to the foliage, the flowers of a tree are a temporary feature and often of rather short duration, but they can be very decorative when open. If borne before the leaves unfold in the spring, such as those of *Magnolia kobus* or the catkins of the goat willow, *Salix caprea*, they are particularly striking. Other trees carry the flowers with the developing leaves, like *Prunus* 'Umineko', or later in the summer, like *Cornus kousa*, or even in the autumn, like *Ligustrum lucidum*. It is possible to choose trees

With its drooping branches and silvery willow-like leaves, *Pyrus salicifolia* 'Pendula' is the most ornamental of the pears

Above left: 'Lutescens', a cultivar of the native whitebeam, *Sorbus aria*; the silvery effect of the foliage helps to compensate for the shade which it casts

Above right: the popular *Acer negundo* 'Variegatum' is particularly effective when hung with winged fruits, but is inclined to lose its variegation

Below left: *Magnolia × loebneri* 'Leonard Messel', a hybrid of *M. kobus*, bears purplish pink flowers in April, before the leaves appear

Below right: sometimes known as the coral bark maple from the strikingly coloured young stems, *Acer palmatum* 'Senkaki' also has delicate yellow green leaves

Opposite: *Robinia pseudoacacia* 'Frisia', with feathery golden yellow foliage in summer, is a fine specimen tree for a town garden

to bloom in succession from February to November, although the majority flower in spring. A number of them, including cherries, crab apples and mahonias, have the bonus of a pleasant scent.

Fruit. Trees normally ripen their fruits in autumn, although many *Prunus* do so in early summer. There are numerous trees which may be grown for the beauty of their fruits, notably rowans, whitebeams and hollies, and also of course for eating. (Fruit trees as such are not covered in this book; see *The Fruit Garden Displayed* for details of these).

Bark and twigs. Some trees are valuable for their ornamental barks or twigs, often most apparent in winter when the twigs have ripened to their distinctive colours and the leaves have been shed. The winter twigs of *Acer palmatum* 'Senkaki' are coral-red, while those of several willows are covered with a greyish green waxy bloom. The snow gum, *Eucalyptus niphophila*, and a number of birches have white barks and the paperbark maple, *Acer griseum*, has a flaking bark of rich reddish brown.

SCREENING

Apart from their own beauty, many trees have a screening function in gardens, visually separating two areas. It is important to decide what sort of screen is required. Too often, trees which grow to 100 ft (30 m) tall are planted where a height of 20 ft (6 m) would be sufficient, perhaps between the bedroom windows of neighbouring two-storey houses. The ubiquitous Leyland cypress, × *Cupressocyparis leylandii*, is a notorious offender. A screen between ground-floor windows should only be 10 ft (3 m) high and, between one ground-floor window and a neighbouring first floor one, 15 ft (4.5 m). Planting tall-growing trees in these situations is a recipe for heavy shade, general aggravation and unnecessary work. Choose trees which fit the bill, like common holly or the Lawson cypress, even if they take one or more years to reach the desired height, and forget about Leyland cypress – it has no place in a small garden.

Sometimes, deciduous trees can be as effective for screening as evergreens, with the winter tracery of the branches preventing through vision and leading the eye away. They are useful too if the screening is needed only during the summer, for instance, to provide privacy for sunbathing. Hawthorn, whitebeam or even hazel might be good choices.

SUPPORT FOR CLIMBERS

Any tree or large shrub can be used as a support for climbing plants, such as *Clematis montana*, variegated ivy, *Rosa filipes* 'Toby Tristram' or *Wisteria sinensis*. This is a good way to grow large climbers which do not sit well on a trellis, so long as they are not prone to diseases and do not need pampering with pruning to produce flowers. It can also be applied to fruit trees where the fruit crop is superfluous, although if you wish to pick most of the fruit, I recommend a non-prickly climber.

SHELTER FOR WILDLIFE

Trees inevitably attract birds and other wildlife to a garden, adding yet another dimension to the pleasure derived from them. They provide shelter in winter, especially conifers, nesting places in spring and food in the form of fruits, seeds or foliage-eating insects.

The Tibetan cherry, *Prunus serrula*, a vigorous small tree valued for the polished bark

Practical considerations

POSITIONING TREES

Trees should be placed where they can be seen to best advantage. Generally, and especially in a restricted space, a tree looks better if it is at the end of an open expanse rather than in the centre. In a front or back garden, this would be near the boundary.

Boundaries. However, a tree must never be positioned directly on a boundary, as this can cause problems when the crown or system of branches develops on the far side. If someone is harmed by a tree overhanging the pavement from your garden, you may be liable for damages. Similarly, your neighbour has the right to remove any branches intruding into his or her garden and may cut them back to the boundary, but no further. The offending material is technically trespassing, although it remains the property of the owner, to whom it should be given back, and cannot be used without permission. Thus to pick overhanging fruit is theft.

Finally, do not place a tree immediately in front of a window but to the side, which is much better in the long term.

Foundations and drains. There are other possible disadvantages of having trees in a garden, apart from shade and root competition with other plants, which should be considered before planting. If the roots of a tree grow beneath the footings of a wall, they can lift or 'jack-up' the wall as they expand, and lead to cracking. This often happens to low walls with very scanty foundations, but rarely to a house. The remedy is to plant the tree some distance from the wall. With small trees, there is little risk if they are kept at least 3 ft (1 m) away.

Some trees, especially willows, can grow in a drain and block it. However, this does not occur unless the drain is already fractured or the joints are poor and it is rarely serious. When planting over or near the run of a weak drain, a precaution would be to choose a tree which is not likely to grow in such wet conditions and prefers dry sandy soils.

In extreme cases, trees may cause subsidence of the foundations of a house. However, this only happens during a dry summer on certain clay subsoils, which shrink as they dry out, and is more of a problem in areas of low rainfall, including southeast England. Provided the house has adequate foundations, small trees can usually be safely planted at a distance of 16 ft (5 m) from them. If you are concerned, advice should be sought either from your local authority or from a qualified arboricultural consultant.

Ultimate size. Trees do not conveniently reach a given size and then cease, for while they live, they grow. However, as they approach maturity and start to flower and fruit profusely, they will slow down, most small trees eventually growing only 2 to 6 in. (5–15 cm) a year in height and radius. The smaller the estimated maximum height of the tree, the slower it is likely to grow and therefore some compromise has to be made between the need for instant or quick effect and long-term value. Most of the trees discussed on pp.34–58 should not grow too large for 20 to 25 years, but a few like *Cedrus deodara* will do so after 15 years. It is a personal decision whether you wish to enjoy such trees temporarily and commit yourself to felling them in about 20 years' time.

THE NATURE OF THE SITE

For further details of individual trees and their preference for or intolerance of certain conditions, see the descriptions on pp.34–58 and the table on pp.60–62.

Soil. Trees will adapt to a wide range of conditions and it is always possible to find suitable ones for difficult soils which are wet or waterlogged, over chalk or limestone, or dry and sandy. Only a few trees have positive dislikes. A good loam, containing a blend of clay, silt and sand particles with a sprinkling of organic matter, will ensure the best growth and the largest trees, but reasonable results can be obtained where there is a least 6 in. (15 cm) of top soil – that is, the upper soil layer, which is rich in nutrients, organic matter and earthworms.

The type of soil does, however, have a marked effect on the rate of establishment and growth. Thus many trees will grow satisfactorily on heavy clay soils which tend to be wet, but on very sticky clays they may take several seasons before starting to make significant new growth. Either this has to be accepted, or the process must be speeded up, by choosing a larger specimen in the first place or by improving the soil. Alternatively, the tree can be planted on a small mound for better drainage.

Both heavy clay and light sandy soils can be improved by adding organic matter in the form of well rotted compost or

Opposite: the deodar, *Cedrus deodara*, is much more attractive as a young tree, when it is dense and shapely with the hanging branch tips

Above: the bay tree, *Laurus nobilis*, a native of the Mediterranean region, thrives in coastal conditions, but may be damaged by frost

Below: even at an early age, *Catalpa bignonioides* 'Aurea' has very large leaves and a naturally low and spreading habit

manure and, if necessary, by putting in drainage to carry water away from the site. Compacted soil is a common problem, especially on land surrounding newly built houses where earthmoving machinery has been used. In a small garden, the most practical method to overcome this and produce a loose open soil, which is beneficial to growth, is double digging. This involves digging to a depth of two spits or spade depths. The first spit (topsoil) is put aside, then the subsoil is dug over and covered with topsoil.

Climate. Despite considerable variation in climate over the length of Britain, many of the trees suitable for small gardens will thrive throughout the country. However, there are some, such as *Arbutus unedo* and *Laurus nobilis*, which are hardy only in the milder districts of southern and western Britain and may require winter protection or the shelter of a wall, particularly in the colder east and north. Unpredictable spring frosts are a general hazard of the British climate, often spoiling young buds or foliage.

Aspect. On the whole, trees prefer an open aspect with full sunlight to grow, flower and fruit well, but will tolerate some shade or being in shadow for part of the day. In dense shade, the choice is more limited, although hollies and cotoneaster, for instance, will flourish. Shade influences the growth of trees, usually making them taller, narrower and more open.

Exposure. Exposure to wind will slow the growth rate and harm the appearance of all trees. Damage is due partly to physical abrasion between twigs and leaves and partly to the drying effect of the wind. Some trees, like *Catalpa bignonioides*, have large floppy leaves which will not stand any battering by the wind, but others, including many pines, willows, rowans and whitebeams, will grow satisfactorily, if more slowly, in exposed situations.

On coasts, exposure tend to be more severe, with nothing to reduce the wind speed as it comes off the sea and salt spray adding to its harmful effects. Nevertheless, some trees, among them juniper and hawthorn, will succeed in these conditions. (See also the Wisley handbook, *Gardening by the sea.*)

Purchasing and planting

TYPES OF TREE

The trees offered by nurseries range from young transplants 1 to 2 ft (30–60 cm) tall, as used in forestry and motorway landscape planting, to semi-mature trees 30–35 ft (10 m) tall, which are appropriate for prestigious developments or instant effect. For owners of small gardens, the choice will probably be confined to trees between 20 in. and 13 ft (0.5–4 m) tall.

Most are sold as standard, half standard or feathered trees. All are from 6½ to 13 ft (2–4 m) tall, with a number of branches in the crown, and have been grown in the nursery for several years. A standard has had the branches removed from the lower 6 ft (1.8 m) of the stem to give a clean stem; in a half standard, the clean stem is shorter, around 3 to 5 ft (1–1.5 m). Both are useful when definite clearance above ground level is needed, or for displaying an attractive bark. On a feathered tree, the small side branches are retained in the nursery, which results in a tree with foliage to the ground. This can be better in natural planting.

Smaller trees, under 6½ ft (2 m), are cheaper to buy and, with proper care, will give as good a return in five years. Less common trees, those which are difficult to transplant and evergreens often have to be acquired at this size.

Trees are available as bare-rooted, root-balled or container-grown plants. Those sold as bare-rooted have been lifted from the ground in the nursery and all the soil shaken off. They should only be bought if the roots are wrapped in damp straw, or similar moisture-retentive material, bound in place by a sheet of polythene or hessian. This is appropriate for deciduous trees, which may be planted during the winter season while dormant.

Root-balled trees have been lifted with the nursery soil attached to the roots, which are usually wrapped in hessian. This can help to ensure the survival of large specimens, trees which are temperamental about transplanting, such as birches, and evergreens. However, it makes them awkward to move and they must be handled carefully to avoid damaging the root ball. They are also more expensive and not generally recommended for private gardens.

Container-grown trees are potted up into a container about a year before being put on sale. The advantages are that the tree should not suffer any check from loss of roots, as it does when lifted, and that it can be planted at any time of year, not just in the winter planting season. This explains why trees from garden centres are normally container-grown, since most of their sales occur in the months of April to June. Evergreens and trees with thick fleshy roots can also be more safely planted if container-grown. A tree which has spent less than three months in the pot should not be purchased, because the roots will not have grown into the compost and this will fall away during planting. A tree which has been in the same pot for two years or more should also be rejected, as it will probably be pot-bound. This happens when the roots become cramped and grow round the pot; once planted, they will continue to do so, rather than spreading out into the soil and forming a strong root system. Such trees rarely thrive and often collapse or are blown down after a few seasons.

Many trees, particularly selected forms which will not come true from seed, are in fact grafted on to a rootstock of the same or a related species.

WHEN AND WHERE TO BUY

Trees can be obtained from nurseries in person, or by mail order if they are reputable firms, from garden centres and from the plant sales outlets of gardens open to the public – often a good source of the unusual. Generally, bare-rooted trees should be purchased and planted only during the period November to early March. Container-grown trees may be bought at other times, although it is wise to avoid the midsummer months, July and August, when they will be growing vigorously and need frequent watering.

PLANTING

The first stage in planting a tree is to excavate a hole or pit. This should be dug at least 6 in. (15 cm) larger in each direction than the spread of the roots or the size of the container. The bottom of the pit should be forked over and the surfaces of the sides should also be broken if these are compacted or glazed, to allow the roots of the tree to spread and penetrate the surrounding soil without diffi-culty. Loose soil should then be placed back in the pit, so that it is as deep as the depth of the roots of the tree, but no more: trees are planted, not buried! Peat or compost can be added to this soil, making up about a quarter of the volume. Peat is particularly advisable for a container-grown tree, which will have been growing in a peat mixture, and it will help the roots adjust to the new conditions. If a stake if required, it should be driven in at this stage, in order not to damage the roots of the tree (see p.25).

When planting in a lawn, turf should be removed from the area of the pit and either used elsewhere or put in the bottom of the pit. It should not be placed on the surface of the soil around the tree, as the grass and weeds will grow, even upside down, and compete for moisture and nutrients to the detriment of the tree.

The roots of a bare-rooted tree should be unwrapped from their protective covering and spread out in the hole. Any that are badly damaged or broken can be cut out, but the root system should be reduced as little as possible. Work the soil between the roots and gently firm in each layer with the foot, taking care not to injure the roots or to stamp on them. Continue until the soil level is the same as that in the nursery, which will show as a dark mark on the bark.

The roots of a container-grown tree may be circling the bottom of the pot, in which case they should either be teased out or the outer spiral should be cut at three or four points, going no deeper into the compost than $\frac{1}{2}$ in. (1 cm), so that new spreading roots are formed. If the plant is pot-bound, with very woody circling roots, it should be returned to the supplier.

A root-balled tree should be placed in the pit before untying the hessian and cutting away at the sides. Any hessian beneath the root ball can be left to rot away.

If the weather prevents immediate planting, trees should be kept in a cool shed until conditions improve. Container-grown and properly packed bare-rooted trees will not suffer, so long as the roots do not dry out.

WATERING

All trees benefit from being watered immediately after planting. This often causes the soil to settle slightly and the next day, after the water has drained, it is sensible to firm the soil again around the tree. Even in the winter, newly planted trees should be watered during dry periods. Watering is especially important with evergreens, which continue to lose moisture from the leaves but may be unable to replace it from the surrounding soil until root growth starts in early spring. Spraying their foliage with water once or twice a day for a fortnight is also helpful, particularly for non-container-grown evergreens planted in late spring and early autumn. However, it is no substitute for keeping the soil moist but not waterlogged.

PROTECTION

Some form of temporary shelter will aid the establishment of trees when they are planted in full leaf with bare roots or poor root

Above left: *Chamaecyparis nootkatensis* 'Pendula', with distinctive long drooping branchlets

Above right: the Himalayan birch, *Betula utilis*, displays its bark to advantage when planted alone on a lawn

Below right: the large decorative fruits of *Malus × robusta* 'Red Siberian' persist well into winter

Figure 1: a newly planted tree with a stake to keep the roots firm and the soil built up in layers

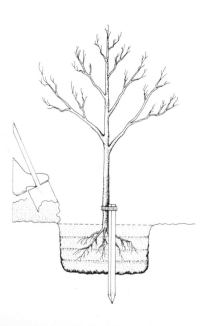

balls, for example, evergreens during winter, or on very exposed sites. A hessian screen may be used, or a large polythene bag, which must be open at both top and bottom otherwise the heat generated by the sun will kill the tree. Similar protection can be given in subsequent winters to trees which are tender when young, such as *Arbutus* and *Eucryphia*.

STAKING

Small trees of less than $3\frac{1}{4}$ ft (1 m) should not require staking except on very windy sites. Trees 3 to 6 ft (1–2 m) tall may need some support and here a bamboo cane will suffice. The tree should be secured to the cane with plastic tape, which expands in hot weather and is pliable, not with wire or string, which cuts into the tree as it grows and does not rot or yield.

For larger trees of $6\frac{1}{2}$ ft (2 m) or more, staking may be necessary. The role of a stake is to hold the roots firm while the tree gets established. The traditional wisdom was to have the stake the same height as the tree, but although this prevents rocking, it is bad for the development of the stem. The stem serves two functions: a small part of it contains tissues which transport water and nutrients between the roots and the crown; most of it is devoted to keeping the top of the tree above the ground where it belongs. Any bending of the stem caused by the wind enables the tree to determine the amount of wood required for purposes of support. However, if a tree is held rigid by a solid stake, the stem does not bend and little structural wood is made. The stem may even be deformed and become greater in diameter above the top tie than it is nearer the ground, instead of being shaped in a desirable steady taper. The consequence is that when the stake is removed or breaks, the tree cannot sustain the crown and falls over.

A short stake about 3 ft (1 m) long will achieve the objective of securing the tree while the roots grow into the soil and will let the stem thicken naturally. Having dug the planting hole, the stake should be driven in near the centre, close to where the stem will be, and should extend approximately 12 to 20 in. (30–50 cm) above soil level. The tree is then planted and attached to it with a plastic tree tie placed at the top of the stake. If the stem itself needs support – and a thin-stemmed tree like *Malus* often does – a bamboo cane should be used in addition. The stake can usually be removed after the second winter, preferably in spring as the tree is about to come in to leaf, and the cane can be taken away at the same time (see figure 1, opposite).

Maintenance

ESTABLISHING A NEWLY PLANTED TREE

The main essential in establishing a newly planted tree, provided it has been properly planted, is to ensure that it does not die from want of moisture during the first couple of seasons. Water can, and should, be given during dry periods in the summer, when at least 4 gallons (15 l) should be applied to the soil immediately around the tree once a week. However, it is much more important to supply the plant with adequate moisture before the soil has dried out, not after. Control of competing weeds is the most effective way of doing this and also allows the tree alone to utilize the nutrients available in the soil, which increases early growth and in itself hastens establishment.

Weeds can be kept in check by traditional means such as hoeing and hand weeding, by using chemical herbicides such as glyphosate (available to amateurs as Tumbleweed), or by applying a mulch. This can be of bark, peat, leaf-mould or other organic matter, or of thick black polythene. The mulch is best put on in the spring, before the ground has become dry, in a layer about 2 in. (5 cm) deep, and will also help to conserve moisture. Whichever method is followed, an area of at least 11 sq. ft (1 m²) around the tree should be kept free of weeds and competing plants, especially grass and clover, for the first two years.

FEEDING

In most gardens, trees do not require fertilizing. However, growth may be enhanced by using either a mulch of well rotted compost or manure, or a chemical fertilizer. A general purpose fertilizer, with an analysis of around 7 to 10 parts each of nitrogen, phosphorus and potassium, is appropriate, at a rate of 2 oz per sq. yd (67 g per m²).

With a young tree it is especially important to apply fertilizer to clean earth, which is free from grass and weeds, otherwise they and not the tree will benefit and make the increased growth; the tree may even be set back as a result of greater competition. With a mature tree, fertilizer can be placed in holes drilled in the ground. It may also be scattered on the soil surface, weeds and all, and will probably work down to the roots within a year or so, provided any grass cuttings are left to rot and not collected.

PRUNING

In a small garden, pruning may be necessary at two stages – first to form a young tree of the desired habit and, second, to control the growth of a mature tree.

Formative pruning. Any weak or crossing branches must be removed, as they will die or rub together, permitting the entry of disease and decay. Certain trees naturally develop a single leader or main stem, which can be seen as a continuation of the trunk, but surplus leaders sometimes arise. These should be cut off when the tree is small, before its appearance is spoilt and it becomes weakened. Similarly, on trees where a clear stem or specified ground clearance is required, unwanted side branches should be removed, including low feathers, before they grow too large.

It is important to carry out formative pruning while the tree is still young and small: a cut only 1 in. (2–3 cm) in diameter will heal more quickly and leave less of a scar than one 4 in. (10 cm) in diameter. Branches should be cut off at the base, just outside the collar of growth.

With variegated trees, any shoots which revert and produce normal green foliage should be cut out below the point of reversion. Apart from destroying the effect of the tree, the green portion tends to grow faster than the variegated part and can quickly take over.

Pruning mature trees. Larger trees can be kept within bounds to some extent by pruning. This is never entirely satisfactory, but may be preferable to removing the tree and waiting for a replacement to grow. Most trees will make new growth if simply hacked but this is not recommended. It encourages disease, results in poorer production of flowers and fruit and leads to excessive regrowth, which often means that the tree is as large or as dense as before within three or four years and looks ugly in winter without the leaves.

Where it is necessary to prune a tree, the object should be to diminish the density or spread of the foliage as unobtrusively as possible. The first can be achieved by removing surplus branches, which are cut off where they join the stem or the main branch. Cuts should be made at a point just outside the collar formed around the base of the branch, in such a way as to prevent the weight of the branch tearing off a strip of bark (see figure 2, p.31). The spread can also be reduced, without destroying the overall shape, by shortening long branches. Where there is a side branch or fork in the branch, the larger portion is cut off, leaving the tree

27

Above: *Cornus controversa* 'Variegata', a small tree of elegant and unusual shape with the bonus of variegated foliage

Below: the great white cherry, *Prunus* 'Tai Haku', may grow up to 25 feet (7.5 m) high and more in width; it flowers in April

Opposite: normally a large upright shrub, *Corylopsis veitchiana* produces fragrant primrose yellow blossom in April and has purplish young leaves

with a similar outline but a smaller spread. Current research shows that tree paints and wound dressings are of very little benefit and best avoided. Neatly sawn wounds will generally heal more quickly if left bare (see figure 3, opposite).

Pruning may be carried out at any season on most trees, with a few exceptions. Cherries are best pruned in midsummer, as there is less risk of infection by silver-leaf disease and of the tree producing a lot of gum. Birches and maples should also be pruned in summer and may bleed badly if cut during the period from midwinter until they are in full leaf. On the whole, if trees are being cut back hard, it is wiser to do this early in the year, when new growth will quickly follow, rather than in late summer, when any subsequent regrowth may not be hardy enough to withstand early autumn frosts. This applies especially to evergreen trees. With conifers, it is important not to cut back into dead brown foliage and to ensure that green leaves are present on the shoots below the cuts, in order for new growth to occur.

Root suckers sometimes appear on grafted trees and can be a problem, as they will often grow faster than the intended top. They should be severed with a spade where they arise from the underground root or stem. Suckers on the bole or lower trunk should be rubbed out in early summer while they are still soft.

Damage caused by the weather should be repaired. Branches broken by wet snow or storms should be cut back to sound side branches and any parts of branches or twigs harmed by cold or frost should be removed. Be cautious, however. The foliage of many evergreen trees can appear badly damaged and brown without the tree suffering any significant injury and it is always sensible to wait until summer to see if the tree is coming into leaf.

TRAINING SHRUBS AS TREES

The distinction between a tree and a shrub is not always clear cut. A number of taller-growing plants, which are commonly regarded as shrubs, can be trained to make a single stem and look like small trees. The process tends to be slower than with true trees, but a shrub treated in this way can be useful as a replacement for a tree which has outgrown its space.

The principle is to select a vigorous vertical shoot to form the main stem and to cut out any competing growths. The stem may need to be held upright with a cane and any shoots arising from the base should be removed, preferably at an early stage in their growth before they become woody.

Some suitable shrubs are listed on p.63 and a few others are mentioned on pp.34–58.

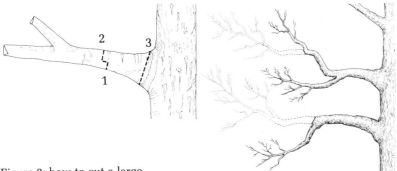

Figure 2: how to cut a large branch – 1) first, make the undercut to stop the bark tearing; 2) next, cut above that to remove the branch; 3) finally, tidy up the stump

Figure 3: top, cutting back to a fork; below, removing a surplus branch

'Red Cascade', a particularly free-fruiting cultivar of the native spindle tree *Euonymus europaeus*

PESTS AND DISEASES

Trees can be afflicted with a number of pests and diseases, but fortunately these are rarely a serious problem, more often simply a nuisance.

The chief pests are aphids, scale insects and caterpillars, which feed mainly on buds, leaves and shoots and can be troublesome or, on young trees, positively harmful. However, they may be dealt with by spraying insecticide, or by applying a tar oil winter wash when growth is fully dormant. Such measures should also help prevent the development of sooty mould, which is caused by sap-feeding insects, while mildews and other diseases may often be controlled by using a fungicide. Two of the most devastating diseases are honey fungus and fireblight and, if symptoms of these are suspected, it is wise to seek expert advice. Otherwise, good general hygiene in the garden, correct planting and after-care and careful pruning should help to keep trees healthy and reasonably free from pests and diseases.

Young trees can be damaged by rabbits gnawing the bark or by cats sharpening their claws on the trunk. Protection can be given with a proprietary tree guard, or one made out of chicken wire or polythene netting. Whatever material is used, it should not constrict or cut into the stem of the tree.

An excellent reference book on this subject, which the reader should consult for further information, is *Collins Guide to the Pests, Diseases and Disorders of Garden Plants*, by Stefan Buczacki and Keith Harris.

A selection of trees for small gardens

This chapter describes some of the many different trees which are suitable for small gardens. The criteria for the selection are that the tree is attractive as a small specimen 13 to 33 ft (4–10 m) tall and that it is reasonably easy to obtain.

Most of the trees discussed are widely available from garden centres, as well as from the larger mail order suppliers. However, a few may need searching for in specialist nurseries or plant sales outlets attached to gardens open to the public. I hope that mentioning these less common ones will encourage gardeners to plant a greater range of trees, rather than relying on just a few which, while excellent in themselves, can be tiresome when over-used.

It must be emphasized that the height of a tree depends both on its inherent character and on the conditions of the site where it is growing. Trees will grow taller on good soils than they will on poor soils. They also tend to be lower and more spreading when grown in full sunlight or an exposed position, but taller and narrower when in heavy shade. All these factors, together with the size of the tree at the time of planting, should be borne in mind when referring to the likely heights indicated in the descriptions below.

The trees are treated in alphabetical order of genus, although within each genus species and forms are often grouped according to similarities. If the tree is evergreen or semi-evergreen, this fact is noted, otherwise it is deciduous.

A descriptive word for the habit – i.e. fastigiate (or narrowly columnar), upright, conical, spreading, domed, weeping – is given at the end of the entry, followed by two sets of figures, showing the estimated height and the diameter of the crown after 10 years and after 20 to 25 years respectively. Types of soil are mentioned only when a tree is intolerant of a particular soil or when it is especially useful on a difficult soil.

Further guidance on choosing trees for specific purposes or situations will be found in the table on pp.60–62, which summarizes the requirements and features of the trees discussed in this chapter. Satisfactory small trees can also be made from a number of the taller-growing shrubs (see p.31).

Abies The silver firs make narrow, crowned, upright, evergreen trees with rather spaced or whorled branching and are usually available as small plants less than $3\frac{1}{4}$ ft (1 m) tall. They are not long-lived on dry or chalky soils.

A. koreana (Korean fir) has blue-green cones, which are freely carried on small trees, and short leaves of vivid silver on the undersides. Conical; $6\frac{1}{2} \times 5$ ft (2×1.5 m); 16×10 ft (5×3 m).

A. forrestii has much larger cones of a brighter violet-blue, but these are not produced on such young trees. The leaves are longer and also bright silver beneath, set on reddish shoots. Conical; $13 \times 6\frac{1}{2}$ ft (4×2 m); 33×13 ft (10×4 m).

A. concolor (Colorado fir) is useful for its fine blue or grey foliage and will thrive on drier sites than the other two, although it will probably grow too large after 15 years. Conical; 23×10 ft (7×3 m); 46×16 ft (14×5 m).

Acer Maples are not generally noticeable for the flowers, but most display good autumn foliage and several have decorative barks.

A. capillipes is one of the snakebark maples, so called because of the white or pale stripes which snake up the otherwise green bark. The winter shoots are bright red and the slightly lobed, glossy leaves turn orange and scarlet in autumn. Spreading; 20×13 ft (6×4 m); 33×20 ft (10×6 m).

Three related species of similar habit are: *A. davidii*, with the bark having brighter white markings, although less reliable autumn colour; *A. grosseri* var. *hersii*, with a beautiful bark and foliage turning red or yellow; and *A. pensylvanicum* (moosewood), with a handsome bark and large leaves becoming yellow in autumn.

A. cappadocicum (Caucasian maple): 'Aureum' has leaves of pale bright yellow when they emerge, slowly changing to green after a few weeks and assuming a brilliant gold in autumn. Domed; $10 \times 6\frac{1}{2}$ ft (3×2 m); 20×13 ft (6×4 m).

A. griseum (paperbark maple) has fiery red autumn colour and a bark of bright red-brown, which is shed in small paper-thin sheets and gives an attractive shaggy appearance, especially in winter. Upright dome; $10 \times 6\frac{1}{2}$ ft (3×2 m); 16×10 ft (5×3 m).

A. japonicum (fullmoon maple) develops brilliant scarlets, golds and purples in autumn. Upright; 10×5 ft (3×1.5 m); 20×10 ft (6×3 m).

A. negundo (box elder): 'Variegatum' has leaves irregularly margined with a broad white zone, giving a marbled effect, but it is inclined to revert to pure green. Spreading; 26×16 ft (8×5 m); 36×26 ft (11×8 m). (See p.12.)

A. palmatum (Japanese maple) is normally grown in the form of one its numerous cultivars, most often sold as small plants around $3\frac{1}{4}$–5 ft (1–1.5 m) tall. They can be damaged by winter cold in exposed situations and are not suitable for shallow chalk soils. Domed; $10 \times 6\frac{1}{2}$ ft (3×2 m); 20×16 ft (6×5 m). 'Atropurpureum' has bright purple new foliage which is somewhat overwhelming in midsummer but turns crimson-purple in autumn. 'Osakazuki' has green leaves which in autumn adopt a series of attractive hues over several weeks, finally turning a brilliant flame-scarlet. 'Senkaki' has smaller leaves becoming yellow in autumn and the one-year-old shoots are coral-red in winter. (See p.12.)

A. pseudoplatanus (sycamore): 'Brilliantissimum' has new leaves which emerge shrimp-pink, changing through yellow or orange to a marbled green. 'Prince Handjery' is similar, with the leaves tinged purple beneath. Domed; $6\frac{1}{2} \times 3\frac{1}{4}$ ft (2×1 m); $10 \times 6\frac{1}{2}$ ft (3×2 m).

Aesculus Horse chestnut

A. neglecta 'Erythroblastos' has new leaves of bright pink, turning to yellow and then green. The young foliage can be damaged by spring frosts. Upright; $10 \times 6\frac{1}{2}$ ft (3×2 m); 16×10 ft (5×3 m).

Alnus Alder

A. incana (grey alder): 'Aurea' has softly yellow leaves and yellow shoots which

Above: *Abies koreana*, like most of the silver firs, prefers a rich moist soil but is tolerant of shade

Below: *Acer japonicum* does best in a moist well drained position away from cold winds

become orange over winter. The male catkins are a rich red, changing to orange-red when expanded in early spring. Upright; 16 × 6½ ft (5 × 2 m); 26 × 13 ft (8 × 4 m). 'Pendula' is similar but weeping; 16 × 13 ft (5 × 4 m); 20 × 20 ft (6 × 6 m). Both forms will grow equally well on wet and dry soils, less so on chalky ones.

Aralia
A. elata (devil's walking stick, Japanese angelica tree) carries enormous compound leaves and bears large clusters of white flowers in September. It is not suitable for gardens frequented by young children, as the stems and leaves are covered with small stout spines. Suckers appear from the base which should be removed to prevent it becoming too shrubby. Domed; 16 × 10 ft (5 × 3 m); 26 × 16 ft (8 × 5 m).

Arbutus
A. unedo (strawberry tree) has small dark leaves and bears ivory-white flowers in small clusters in October and November. The strawberry-like fruits ripen the following autumn and are edible but unpalatable. It is evergreen and young plants need winter protection in exposed gardens. Domed; 10 × 6½ ft (3 × 2 m); 16 × 10 ft (5 × 2 m).

Betula Birches are planted for the attractive bark, the delicate and often light foliage, the male catkins with the leaves in spring and the autumn colour. They must have an open situation, as they do not tolerate shade. They have aggressive surface roots and few plants can be grown satisfactorily beneath them.

B. medwediewii has light yellow leaves in autumn, with glossy brown shoots and large buds in winter. Domed; 8 × 6½ ft (2.5 × 2 m); 16 × 16 ft (5 × 5 m).

B. nigra (river birch) has a shaggy, pinkish orange bark and will tolerate wet soils. Upright; 13 × 6½ ft (4 × 2 m); 26 × 13 ft (8 × 4 m).

B. pendula (silver birch): 'Dalecarlica' has drooping branches and deeply cut leaves. Upright; 26 × 10 ft (8 × 3 m); 49 × 16 ft (15 × 5 m). 'Youngii' makes a cascading mound, usually not growing taller than the height of the stem on to which it was grafted in the nursery. Weeping; 10 × 10 ft (3 × 3 m); 13 × 20 ft (4 × 6 m).

B. utilis (Himalayan birch) has a bark which ranges in colour from mahogany to dazzling white. The trees with very white barks are usually listed as *B. jacquemontii*. Upright; 20 × 6½ ft (6 × 2 m); 39 × 16 ft (12 × 5 m). (See p.24.) 'Sauwala White' is smaller, with a very white bark; 13 × 6½ ft (4 × 2 m); 26 × 23 ft (8 × 4 m).

Calocedrus
C. decurrens (incense cedar) is an evergreen conifer of distinctive columnar shape, with fans of bright green foliage. Unlike the related cypresses, it is resistant to honey fungus. Fastigiate; 16 × 3¼ ft (5 × 1 m); 36 × 6½ ft (11 × 2 m). (See p.38.)

Carpinus Hornbeam
C. turczaninowii has small densely borne leaves which turn russet in autumn and it thrives on heavy clay soils. Upright; 10 × 6½ ft (3 × 2 m); 20 × 13 ft (6 × 4 m).

Catalpa
C. bignonioides (Indian bean tree) produces large panicles of spotted white flowers in July and the heart-shaped leaves are up to 10 in. (24 cm) across. Spreading; 20 × 10 ft (6 × 3 m); 30 × 20 ft (9 × 6 m). 'Aurea' has bright yellow foliage, fading towards the end of summer and when grown in shade, but does not flower; 13 × 10 ft (4 × 3 m); 20 × 13 ft (6 × 4 m). Neither can withstand exposure and they are only suitable for sheltered locations in the southern half of Britain. (See p.19.)

Cedrus Cedar
C. deodara (deodar) has bluish green foliage and short horizontal branches which are emphatically pendulous at the tips. An evergreen, it will eventually grow too tall, but is very attractive for 15 to 20 years. Upright weeping; 26 × 6½ ft (8 × 2 m); 39 × 13 ft (12 × 4 m). (See p.18.)

Cercidiphyllum
C. japonicum (Katsura tree) has delicate, small, heart-shaped leaves which are bright pink when young and assume a rich variety of autumn tints in favourable

seasons. The new leaves may be damaged by spring frosts, but the tree will produce fresh ones. Upright; 23 × 10 ft (7 × 3 m); 39 × 20 ft (12 × 6 m). (See p.64)

Cercis
C. siliquastrum (Judas tree) carries abundant clusters of purple flowers in May, emerging from buds on old wood and often from the trunk itself. It is adapted to hot dry locations and will thrive on chalk or limestone. Domed; 10 × 6½ ft (3 × 2 m); 16 × 10 ft (5 × 3 m). (See p.39.)
C. canadensis (redbud): 'Forest Pansy', of similar shape and size, has striking purple foliage from spring into August and gives bright reddish purple colours in autumn, but is not free-flowering.

Chamaecyparis Cypresses are the most commonly planted evergreen conifers and range from tall trees of 66 ft (20 m) or more to dwarf trees suitable for rock gardens. They are not tolerant of waterlogged soils.
C. lawsoniana (Lawson cypress) produces interesting variations in foliage colour and habit when raised from seed and these make good evergreen screens without growing too tall too fast. Fastigiate or upright; 13 × 3¼ ft (4 × 1 m); 33–49 × 10–16 ft (10–15 × 3–5 m). Named forms, which are usually planted as specimen trees, also provide a range of different shapes and tree colours. They include 'Allumii', spire-like with bluish foliage; 'Columnaris', with paler grey-blue foliage and columnar habit; 'Kilmacurragh', very narrowly fastigiate with bright green leaves; 'Lane' and 'Stewartii', with golden yellow foliage sprays; and 'Pembury Blue', with bright blue-grey leaves in pendulous sprays on a broadly conical tree.
C. nootkatensis 'Pendula' has an open crown of level branches with foliage hanging vertically in flat sprays. Conical weeping. (See p.24.)
C. obtusa (Hinoki cypress): 'Crippsii' has bright gold foliage. Conical; both 8 × 3 ft (2.5 × 1 m); 20 × 10 ft (6 × 3 m).

Cornus The dogwoods are a large genus which includes several small trees.
C. controversa (table dogwood) has remarkable level tiers of foliage on horizontal branches and large clusters of creamy white flowers carried above these in June. 'Variegata' is an exquisite slower-growing form, with the leaves margined creamy white. Upright conical; 16 × 6½ ft (5 × 2 m); 23 × 10 ft (7 × 3 m). (See p.28.)
C. kousa var. *chinensis* has flowers surrounded by four large creamy white bracts and borne above the foliage in June on horizontal branches. These are followed by edible strawberry-like fruits and attractive red-tinted dying leaves in autumn. Upright conical; 10 × 6½ ft (3 × 2 m); 20 × 10 ft (6 × 3 m). (See p.41.)

Corylus Hazel
C. avellana, the native hazel, is often grown for its edible nuts. It has fresh yellow catkins hanging from the branches in late winter and the leaves turn russet in autumn. It tends to be shrubby, with many stems and suckers arising from the base, but is useful for screening. Domed; 13 × 13 ft (4 × 4 m); 20 × 20 ft (6 × 6 m).

Cotoneaster
C. 'Cornubia' is semi-evergreen and has small, white, hawthorn-scented flowers in summer, its chief glory being the profusion of large red berries in autumn. Spreading; 16 × 10 ft (5 × 3 m); 26 × 20 ft (8 × 6 m). *C. frigidus* is very similar, with larger leaves. Both need pruning and training to one stem when young to develop as trees (see p.30).
C. glaucophyllus is more of a spreading shrub and more fully evergreen. The leaves are greyish blue beneath and the small fruits are orange-red, colouring late, around Christmas, to give a welcome bonus of colour at that season.

Overleaf: with its narrow habit, *Calocedrus decurrens* is ideal planted as a single specimen or in a group and deserves to be more widely grown

Crataegus Hawthorn

C. monogyna (common hawthorn, may) is initially upright and becomes more spreading, with pendulous tips to the branches. It is wreathed with fragrant white flowers in May, followed by the purplish red haws or fruits; 13 × 6½ ft (4 × 2 m); 23 × 16 ft (7 × 5 m). C. oxycantha 'Paul's Scarlet' has double scarlet flowers. C. prunifolia has glossy leaves which change to rich crimson in autumn. The large red fruits remain on the tree after the leaves are lost.

Cupressus Cypress

C. glabra (smooth cypress) has a smooth reddish or deep purple bark. The yellow male catkins contrast with the evergreen blue foliage in autumn. It is especially suitable for hot, dry or chalky soils. Conical; 16 × 6½ ft (5 × 2 m); 33 × 13 ft (10 × 4 m).

Decaisnea

D. fargesii has stout shoots covered in a waxy bloom and large pinnate leaves (made up of leaflets) nearly 3 ft (90 cm) long. Yellowish green flowers in May are followed by the large, waxy, metallic blue pods in autumn. It is not recommended for sites where spring frosts are common. Upright; 10 × 6½ ft (3 × 2 m); 16 × 13 ft (5 × 4 m).

Embothrium

E. coccineum (fire bush) is a flamboyant tree in May and June when covered in the brilliant crimson-scarlet or orange-scarlet tubular flowers. It is evergreen and will tolerate some shade, but must have a moist acidic soil and a sheltered site. Fastigiate; 20 × 3¼ ft (6 × 1 m); 30 × 5 ft (9 × 1.5 m).

Eucalyptus

E. gunnii (cider gum), a hardy evergreen, will become too large within 10 years if left to grow naturally. It can be cut back to ground level or a short stem annually in spring and will make new growths with bright blue foliage of up to 10 ft (3 m) in a season. Upright; 33 × 10 ft (10 × 3 m); 66 × 26 ft (20 × 8 m). (See p.43.)

E. niphophila (snow gum) is another hardy species, evergreen and slower-growing. It has mahogany-coloured new leaves turning glossy green, twigs which are shiny dark red in winter, becoming covered with a waxy bloom in spring, and a creamy white bark. Domed; 16 × 10 ft (5 × 3 m); 26 × 20 ft (8 × 6 m).

Eucryphia

E. × nymansensis 'Nymansay' has dark green, evergreen leaves showing off the large white flowers, which are profusely borne in August and early September once the tree is a few years old. It will grow on all soils, including chalky ones, but can be tender when young and is not suited to cold northern gardens. Upright; 16 × 3¼ ft (5 × 1 m); 30 × 10 ft (9 × 3 m).

Euonymus Spindle tree

E. europaeus 'Red Cascade' has rosy red fruits on weeping branches, giving a fine autumn effect. Upright; 10 × 3¼ ft (3 × 1 m); 16 × 10 ft (5 × 3 m). (See p.32.)

Fagus Beech

F. sylvatica 'Dawyck' has green foliage, while 'Dawyck Purple' has purple foliage and is slower-growing. Both make effective 'exclamation marks'. Fastigiate; 26 × 3¼ ft (8 × 1 m); 39 × 10 ft (12 × 3 m). 'Purpurea Pendula' grows only as tall as the stem on which it is trained or grafted, forming a complete cascade of purple leaves. Weeping; 10 × 6½ ft (3 × 2 m); 10 × 10 ft (3 × 3 m).

F. engleriana has sea-green foliage and, like other beeches, it will grow on acidic and alkaline sites, but does not tolerate heavy waterlogged soils. Domed; 13 × 6½ ft (4 × 2 m); 23 × 13 ft (7 × 4 m).

Overleaf: as well as the magnificent flowers, Cercis siliquastrum has pretty heart-shaped leaves and, in winter, conspicuous long seed pods; it needs full sun and performs best in southern England

Above: *Cornus kousa* var. *chinensis*, blooming profusely at a time when many trees and shrubs are not in flower, benefits from a sunny position

Below: the spectacular fire bush, *Embothrium coccineum*, was originally introduced from Chile in 1846

Fraxinus Ash

F. mariesii bears creamy white flowers in June, followed in July by deep purple fruits. It will grow on a wide range of soils and deserves to be better known. Domed; $6\frac{1}{2} \times 3\frac{1}{4}$ ft $(2 \times 1$ m$)$; 13×10 ft $(4 \times 3$ m$)$.

F. velutina (Arizona ash) has velvety hairy shoots and leaves, the latter turning yellow in autumn. It is better suited to eastern England or a dry sunny site. Domed; $13 \times 6\frac{1}{2}$ ft $(4 \times 2$ m$)$; 23×13 ft $(7 \times 4$ m$)$.

Genista Broom

G. aetnensis (Mount Etna broom) has slender, almost leafless, green, rather pendulous shoots and is covered with fragrant, yellow, pea-like flowers in July and early August. The green branches give it the appearance of an evergreen. Upright; $16 \times 3\frac{1}{4}–6\frac{1}{2}$ ft $(5 \times 1–2$ m$)$; $23 \times 6\frac{1}{2}–10$ ft $(7 \times 2–3$ m$)$. (See p.44.)

Ginkgo

G. biloba (maidenhair tree) has oily green, fan-shaped, curiously lobed leaves, which assume a beautiful golden yellow colour in late autumn. It will eventually grow too large for most gardens – the tree at Kew, planted in 1762, is now over 70 ft $(21$ m$)$ tall – but as a young tree and for the first half century, it has a very narrow crown with little side branching. Fastigiate; $16 \times 3\frac{1}{4}$ ft $(5 \times 1$ m$)$; $30 \times 3\frac{1}{4}–6\frac{1}{2}$ ft $(9 \times 1–2$ m$)$.

Gleditsia

G. triacanthos (honey locust): 'Sunburst' has feathery pinnate or doubly pinnate foliage (composed of leaflets on each side of the stalk) which is golden yellow in spring and remains a fresh light or yellow green throughout the summer. It makes a very striking tree, better in full sun, although tolerating light shade. Domed; $16 \times 6\frac{1}{2}$ ft $(5 \times 2$ m$)$; 26×13 ft $(8 \times 4$ m$)$.

Halesia

H. monticola (mountain snowdrop tree) bears pendent, white, bell-shaped flowers in May, followed by curiously winged green fruits. Upright; $16 \times 6\frac{1}{2}$ ft $(5 \times 2$ m$)$; 26×13 ft $(8 \times 4$ m$)$. (See p.45.)

Hydrangea

H. paniculata is usually cultivated as a shrub, but can easily be trained into a small tree (see p.30). According to the form grown, conical white panicles of flowers are displayed from July ('Praecox'), through August and September ('Grandiflora'), to September and October ('Tardiva'). Spreading; 16×10 ft $(5 \times 3$ m$)$.

Ilex Hollies are useful for their evergreen foliage and long-persisting berries. Plants are normally either male or female and therefore both must be planted to ensure that the female produces berries. Hollies will grow well in shady locations, but can be difficult to move and are usually only available as small plants. Upright; $10 \times 3\frac{1}{4}$ ft $(3 \times 1$ m$)$; $23 \times 6\frac{1}{2}$ ft $(7 \times 2$ m$)$.

I. aquifolium (common holly) has given rise to many attractive forms, including 'Amber', with numerous orange berries; 'Argentea Pendula', with grey-green leaves having a broad creamy white margin, many red berries and purplish pendulous shoots, which makes a small weeping tree; 'Golden Milkboy', male, with spiny leaves with a yellow centre; 'Handsworth New Silver', female, with leaves edged with cream and the similar 'Silver Queen', male (see p.45); and 'J. C. van Tol', one of the few hermaphrodite plants, which produces prolific red berries when planted on its own.

Eucalyptus gunni, the cider gum, has been recorded as reaching over 100 feet $(30$ m$)$ high, although more often seen as a bushy medium-sized tree

Opposite: *Genista aetnensis* requires no more than a sunny spot and a well-drained soil to succeed and is completely hardy

Above: the mountain snowdrop tree, *Halesia monticola*, grows rapidly and flowers from an early age

Below: the boldly variegated 'Silver Queen', like other forms of *Ilex aquifolium*, adapts to almost any situation and soil

I. × *altaclarensis* (Highclere holly): 'Belgica Aurea' has leaves mottled grey-green with a yellow margin and 'Golden King' has red berries and green leaves splashed with grey and edged with gold.

Juniperus Junipers are usually obtainable as plants less than $3\frac{1}{4}$ ft (1 m) and are not likely to exceed a height of 10 ft (3 m) in 10 years. They are evergreen and especially recommended for hot, dry or chalky sites.

J. chinensis (Chinese juniper) is known in innumerable forms. 'Aurea' (Young's golden juniper) has golden foliage, becoming more pronounced on older plants, and massed yellow cones in April. 'Kaizuka' is a characterful plant, an erratically sprawling bush or small tree with bright green, dense foliage, often loaded with small greyish green berries or cones in autumn. Upright; $10 \times 3\frac{1}{4}$ ft (3×1 m).

J. recurva (Himalayan juniper) has gracefully drooping branchlets, a flaky orange-brown bark and grey-green foliage. The variety *coxii* (coffin juniper) has longer needles of a mid-green colour. Weeping; $10 \times 6\frac{1}{2}$ ft (3×2 m); 16×10 ft (5×3 m).

J. scopulorum 'Skyrocket' is a distinctive pencil-thin tree with blue-grey foliage, the narrow crown usually being one tenth as wide as the plant is tall. It is useful as a punctuation mark in a scheme, or for creating a mini-avenue between two areas. Fastigiate; $13 \times 1\frac{1}{4}$ ft (4×0.4 m); $26 \times 1\frac{1}{2}$ ft (8×0.5 m).

Koelreuteria

K. paniculata (pride of India) has large pinnate leaves consisting of oval leaflets, which turn yellow in autumn. In July and August it is covered in large panicles of numerous small yellow flowers, followed by unusual bladder-like fruits. For best development, it needs a warm sunny position in the southern and eastern parts of the country. Domed; 16×10 ft (5×3 m); 30×20 ft (9×6 m).

Laburnum

L. × *watereri* 'Vossii' bears large hanging racemes of yellow flowers up to 2 ft (60 cm) long in May and early June. It will not tolerate waterlogged soils. Spreading; 23×13 ft (7×4 m); 26×20 ft (8×6 m).

Laurus

L. nobilis (bay laurel) is evergreen and has leathery, dark green, aromatic leaves – the bayleaves used in cooking. Insignificant yellow flowers appear in late April and small black berries in the autumn. It is not fully hardy in central and northern districts, where it is susceptible to damage in severe winters and may be no more than a shrub. However, it will tolerate maritime exposure, and along the south coast grows taller than shown. It can be clipped into shape. Upright; $13 \times 6\frac{1}{2}$ ft (4×2 m); 26×16 ft (8×5 m). (See p.19.)

Ligustrum Privet

L. lucidum (Chinese privet) has glossy evergreen leaves and is valuable for the white flowers borne in large panicles in late August and September. It is quite unlike the generally perceived idea of a privet. 'Excelsum Superbum' is a form in which the leaves are margined and mottled with deep yellow and cream. In 'Tricolor', they have an irregular white border and are pinkish when young. Both are very striking small trees. Conical becoming domed; $13 \times 6\frac{1}{2}$ ft (4×2 m); 26×20 ft (8×6 m).

L. compactum has semi-evergreen lance-shaped leaves up to 6 in. (15 cm) long and is attractive in July when laden with white flowers. Domed; $13 \times 6\frac{1}{2}$ ft (4×2 m); 26×16 ft (8×5 m). *L. chenaultii* is similar, but with leaves to 10 in. (25 cm) long.

Lindera

L. obtusiloba produces yellow flowers in dense clusters on the twigs in March and April. The leaves may be entire or lobed, always prominently three-veined, and turn a fine butter-yellow in autumn. It is an unusual small tree, well worth considering if you want something out of the ordinary. Domed; $13 \times 6\frac{1}{2}$ ft (4×2 m); 23×13 ft (7×4 m).

Magnolia The magnolias have magnificent large flowers with fleshy petal and sepals (collectively called tepals), in some cases emerging before the leaves in spring, when they are susceptible to damage by frosts. The roots are thick and very fleshy, easily rotting if injured, and resent any disturbance or digging around them. Magnolias are best planted in early autumn or late April to May, when the roots are actively growing, and the ones mentioned here grow on most soils, including deep chalky soils. Apart from the flowers, the fruits are often ornamental, especially when opening to reveal the scarlet seeds.

M. *delavayi* is evergreen and has large, dull greyish green leaves up to 14 in. (35 cm) long. The creamy white, fragrant flowers, up to 8 in. (20 cm) across, are borne at the ends of the shoots. They last only a day but are carried in succession from late summer into autumn. Unfortunately, it is hardy only in the milder parts of the country; elsewhere it will be harmed in bad winters and should be grown against the wall of a house for shelter. Domed; 13 × 6½ ft (4 × 2 m); 23 × 13 ft (7 × 4 m).

M. *grandiflora* (bull bay, evergreen magnolia) has large, glossy, yellow-green leaves with rusty hairs beneath. The creamy white flowers, up to 10 in. (25 cm) across, have a spicy scent and are produced in successive flushes from July until the frosts in November. It is evergreen and hardy as a free-standing tree without wall protection in southern and western parts. Domed; 13 × 6½ ft (4 × 2 m); 23 × 13 ft (7 × 4 m).

M. *kobus* has pure white flowers up to 4 in. (10 cm) across. Although slow to bloom when young, after about 12 to 15 years a mature tree may be covered with literally hundreds of flowers in April. Domed; 13 × 6½ ft (4 × 2 m); 23 × 10 ft (7 × 3 m). Two hybrids, M. × *loebneri* 'Leonard Messel' and 'Merrill', make similar small trees but have the virtue of flowering from a young age. (See p.12.)

M. *salicifolia* (willow magnolia) carries the pure white flowers in late April on bare branches. These are less vulnerable to frost damage than those of other early-flowering magnolias and the tree blooms at a young age. Upright; 13 × 5 ft (4 × 1.5 m); 23 × 8 ft (7 × 2.5 m).

M. *virginiana* (sweet bay) is evergreen or deciduous and produces a constant succession of very fragrant, rather small, creamy white, later darkening, flowers from June until September. It is a choice but uncommon tree. Upright or domed; 13 × 5 ft (4 × 1.5 m); 20 × 10 ft (6 × 3 m).

M. *wilsonii* bears scented, white, cup-shaped, hanging flowers in May and June, best seen from below, and gives a further display in September with fruits and seeds. Spreading; 13 × 10 ft (4 × 3 m); 20 × 16 ft (6 × 5 m). M. *sieboldii* is similar, with flowers facing outwards. (See p.48.)

Mahonia

M. 'Charity' has bold, evergreen, prickly leaves and fragrant yellow flowers from October onwards. Although usually planted as a shrub, it grows into a tree with a distinctive ridged bark. Domed; 10 × 6½ ft (3 × 2 m); 23 × 13 ft (7 × 4 m).

Malus Crab

M. *baccata* (Siberian crab) is covered with massed white flowers in April, followed by small bright red or yellow crab-apples, which persist over winter. Spreading dome; 13 × 10 ft (4 × 3 m); 30 × 26 ft (9 × 8 m).

M. *floribunda* (Japanese crab) is bedecked in late April with flowers which are rosy red in bud, opening pale pink, and in autumn with red or yellow berries. Spreading; 10 × 6½ ft (3 × 2 m); 16 × 16 ft (5 × 5 m).

M. 'John Downie' has flowers pink in bud, opening white, and then conical yellow crab-apples 1 in. (3 cm) long, which may be used to make jelly. Upright becoming domed; 16 × 10 ft (5 × 3 m); 26 × 20 ft (8 × 6 m).

M. × *robusta* has white or pinkish flowers, followed by large fruits, red in 'Red Siberian' and yellow in 'Yellow Siberian', which remain into winter. Domed; 13 × 10 ft (4 × 3 m); 20 × 13 ft (6 × 4 m). (See p.24 and p.48.)

M. *transitoria* bears masses of small white flowers in late May and tiny yellow fruits which last long into winter. Spreading; 13 × 13 ft (4 × 4 m); 16 × 23 ft (5 × 7 m).

M. *tschonoskii* (Chonusuki crab) is a useful tree for confined spaces. The foliage

Above: the exotic large blooms of *Magnolia sieboldii* are followed by scarlet fruits and seeds

Below: the flowering crabs, including the familiar *Malus × robusta* 'Yellow Siberian', are undemanding small trees and flourish in all types of soil

Opposite: *Metasequoia glyptostroboides*, the only living representative of a prehistoric genus, was discovered in China in 1947

emerges silvery grey and turns a brilliant mixture of colours in the autumn. Conical; 23 × 10 ft (7 × 3 m); 36 × 20 ft (11 × 6 m).

Metasequoia
M. glyptostroboides (dawn redwood) thrives on both wet and dry soils. On the former it will grow too large after 15 years, but on the latter it slows down appreciably once it has reached 26–33 ft (8–10 m). It has fresh green foliage, becoming red in October and November, and fibrous orange-brown bark. Conical; 26 × 10 ft (8 × 3 m); 39 × 16 ft (12 × 5 m). (See p.49.)

Morus Mulberry
M. nigra (black mulberry) has large heart-shaped leaves and fruits changing from orange-scarlet to blackish purple in midsummer. Ripe mulberries are very tasty, but stain the fingers purple. Domed; 10 × 6½ ft (3 × 2 m); 16 × 16 ft (5 × 5 m).

Nothofagus Southern beech
N. antarctica (Antarctic beech) is a fast-growing tree similar in many respects to beech or birch, with small, usually balsam-scented leaves. It will not grow on chalk soils. Upright; 23 × 10 ft (7 × 3 m); 33 × 16 ft (10 × 5 m).

Nyssa
N. sylvatica (tupelo, black gum) has glossy leaves, which become bright red and yellow in autumn, and downturned branches. It will flourish on moist and acidic soils, but is not suitable for those over chalk. Conical; 13 × 6½ ft (4 × 2 m); 26 × 13 ft (8 × 4 m). (See p.2.)

Picea Spruces are evergreen and are normally available as small trees less than 3 ft (1 m) tall. Any which grows too large can always be felled and the top used as a Christmas tree.
P. breweriana has horizontal side branches curtained with very long pendulous branchlets up to 6½ ft (2 m) in length. Plants which have been grafted should be purchased, as seedling trees take many years to develop this mature foliage. Upright; 10 × 6½ ft (3 × 2 m); 20 × 10 ft (6 × 3 m).
P. omorika (Serbian spruce) has a very narrow crown which, even when the tree ultimately reaches 50 ft (15 m) tall, is only 13 ft (4 m) wide and unlikely to become too spreading. It will grow at the same steady rate on wet, dry, acid or chalk soils. Conical; 16 × 3 ft (5 × 1 m); 26 × 5 ft (8 × 1.5 m).
P. orientalis (oriental spruce): 'Aurea' has very short needles, which are golden yellow for six weeks around June, afterwards turning dark green. The cones are brick-red and very attractive in April. Conical; 16 × 10 ft (5 × 3 m); 26 × 13 ft (8 × 4 m).
P. pungens (Colorado spruce, blue spruce) is invariably grown as one of its many forms, for instance, 'Glauca', 'Koster', 'Hoopsii' and 'Spekii', which have bright blue foliage and silvery blue new growth. A grafted plant may be slow to form an erect leader and the tree should be fed and watered to get it growing vigorously. Aphids cause the loss of needles and can be controlled by spraying with malathion or pirimicarb insecticides, either when the problem is noticed or as a precaution in August. Conical; 10 × 6½ ft (3 × 2 m); 20 × 13 ft (6 × 4 m).

Pinus Pines have relatively long, evergreen leaves or needles, grouped in bundles of from two to five. They are especially suited to dry sandy sites.
P. aristata (bristlecone pine) has dark green needles flecked with white resin and bunched in fives. These are retained for up to 15 years and result in a densely crowned tree. Domed; 8 × 6½ ft (2.5 × 2 m); 16 × 13 ft (5 × 4 m).
P. bungeana (lacebark pine) has a grey-green bark, which peels off in small plates to reveal a creamy or pale yellow colour, gradually darkening to green, olive-brown, red or purple. It has leaves in threes. Conical; 10 × 6½ ft (3 × 2 m); 16 × 10 ft (5 × 3 m).
P. leucodermis (Bosnian pine) has dense, dark green needles in pairs and cones of a rich cobalt-blue in the summer of the second year, ripening to light brown. It is suitable for most soils, including those over chalk. Conical; 13 × 10 ft (4 × 3 m); 26 × 16 ft (8 × 5 m).

P. sylvestris (Scots pine): 'Aurea' has paired leaves which turn bright gold from December until April, the colour being particularly pronounced in cold weather, and for the rest of the year are bluish green. The male cones can be a good lemon-yellow in June. Conical; 13 × 10 ft (4 × 3 m); 26 × 13 ft (8 × 4 m).

Prunus Cherries will grow on a wide range of soils, but are not usually long-lived, especially on sandy or chalky soils. They are easy to transplant and quickly make effective trees.

P. 'Kursar' has vivid pink flowers in March and leaves colouring orange in autumn. Upright; 13 × 6½ ft (4 × 2 m); 20 × 10 ft (6 × 3 m). April flowering are *P.* 'Pandora' which carries shell-pink flowers, while *P.* 'Snow Goose' and *P.* 'Umineko' have white flowers and green new leaves.

P. *maackii* bears white flowers in short racemes in April, but its best feature is the smooth, yellowish brown, peeling bark. Spreading; 16 × 10 ft (5 × 3 m); 26 × 16 ft (8 × 5 m).

P. *sargentii* (Sargent cherry) has pink flowers in early April, with the initially wine-coloured new foliage turning brilliant red in September. Spreading; 16 × 13 ft (5 × 4 m); 26 × 23 ft (8 × 7 m).

P. *serrula* (Tibetan cherry) is grown for the shining, mahogany-coloured, peeling bark. The flowers are small and white, while the leaves are willow-like. Spreading; 16 × 10 ft (5 × 3 m); 23 × 16 ft (7 × 5 m).

P. *subhirtella* has single rose-pink flowers. 'Autumnalis', the autumn cherry, starts to produce its semi-double pink, fading to white flowers in the autumn and continues in a series of flushes over the winter. Spreading; 13 × 10 ft (4 × 3 m); 20 × 16 ft (6 × 5 m). 'Pendula Rosea' and 'Pendula Rubra' bear rose and deep rose flowers in late March and early April. They are weeping and develop a spreading mushroom-like crown up to 13–16 ft (4–5 m) wide.

The Japanese cherries are a group of small trees of hybrid origin, very decorative in flower, but often less so for the remainder of the year. 'Amanogawa', with shell-pink flowers around the end of April, associates well with tulips. Fastigiate; 16 × 3¼ ft (5 × 1 m); 23 × 6½ ft (7 × 2 m). 'Cheal's Weeping Cherry' has deep pink flowers in early April. Weeping; 10–13 ft (3–4 m) × 13–16 ft (4–5 m). 'Kanzan' carries pink double flowers in early May, when it can look glorious, and the foliage turns bronzy orange in autumn. A young tree, being spiky and erect, can appear rather stark, although when older the branches arch out and down. Generally, it is better enjoyed in your neighbour's garden. Upright, then spreading; 16 × 13 ft (5 × 4 m); 30 × 26 ft (9 × 8 m).

'Pink Perfection' bears double rose-pink flowers in mid-May. Upright; 16 × 13 ft (5 × 4 m); 20 × 20 ft (6 × 6 m). 'Shimidsu Sakura' has flowers which are pink in bud and open pure white, hanging from the horizontal branches in early May. Spreading; 13–16 ft (4–5 m) × 16–20 ft (5–6 m). (See cover.) 'Tai Haku' (great white cherry) produces the largest flowers of any Japanese cherry, a dazzling white, single and over 2 in. (6 cm) across. The new leaves are deep red and become yellow or orange in autumn. Spreading; 20 × 20 ft (6 × 6 m); 26 × 30 ft (8 × 9 m). (See p.28.)

Pyrus Pear

P. *salicifolia* 'Pendula' (willow-leaved pear) has silvery willow-like foliage on drooping branches, which arch down and out, and white flowers lost among the leaves. Weeping; 10 × 10 ft (3 × 3 m); 16 × 16 ft (5 × 5 m). (See p.11.)

Quercus Oak

Q. *pontica* (Armenian oak) has large oval leaves up to 8 in. (20 cm) long, with russet autumn colour. Domed; 10 × 10 ft (3 × 3 m); 16 × 16 ft (5 × 5 m).

Overleaf: 'Aurea', a slow-growing golden-leaved cultivar of *Picea orientalis*, is one of the daintiest of the spruces

Rhus Sumach

R. typhina (stag's horn sumach) will easily form a small tree with a little pruning (see p.30). The pinnate leaves with many leaflets give glorious autumn shades of orange, yellow, red and purple, followed by the winter silhouette of the stout hairy branches. Domed; 10 × 10 ft (3 × 3 m); 16 × 20 ft (5 × 6 m).

Robinia Robinias are especially useful for hot, dry or sandy sites, but not water-logged soils. The brittle branches are liable to be broken in exposed situations.

R. kelseyi has graceful pinnate leaves and bright rose-coloured, fragrant flowers in June, followed by bristly pods. Spreading; 10–13 ft × 6½ ft (3–4 × 2 m); 16 × 13 ft (5 × 4 m).

R. pseudoacacia (black locust, false acacia): 'Frisia' is a very distinctive tree with golden yellow foliage. Upright; 26 × 13 ft (8 × 4 m); 39 × 16 ft (12 × 5 m). (See p.13.)

Salix Willows are good for wet situations, although the roots can be a problem if they enter a fractured drain. The trees are valuable for the early catkins.

S. caprea (goat willow, great sallow) bears silvery female catkins – as the well-known pussy willow – or large yellow male ones, in early spring. Upright; 26 × 13 ft (8 × 4 m); 33 × 20 ft (10 × 6 m).

S. daphnoides (violet willow) has one-year-old shoots thickly covered in a waxy bloom, giving a whitish blue effect in winter. Upright; 26 × 16 ft (8 × 5 m); 33 × 20 ft (10 × 6 m).

S. pentandra (bay willow), with glossy green foliage, is unusual among willows in producing the long yellow catkins after the leaves, in June. Upright; 13 × 10 ft (4 × 3 m); 23 × 16 ft (7 × 5 m).

S. purpurea (purple osier) has narrow blue-green leaves. Domed; 13 × 10 ft (4 × 3 m); 16 × 16 ft (5 × 5 m). 'Pendula' is a small weeping form, with long hanging branches on a mound-shaped tree up to 16 ft (5 m) tall. It is the ideal weeping willow for small, and indeed most, gardens. 'Eugenei' is a slender erect form; up to 16 × 6½ ft (5 × 2 m).

Sophora

S. japonica (Japanese pagoda tree): 'Pendula' develops a domed drooping form with highly contorted branches, giving an interesting outline in winter. Weeping; 10 × 10 ft (3 × 3 m); 16 × 16 ft (5 × 5 m). (See p.56.)

Sorbus This large genus includes the rowans, which have pinnate leaves with numerous leaflets, and the whitebeams, which have simple not compound leaves, usually silvery beneath. All thrive on a wide variety of soils and are easily transplanted.

S. aria (whitebeam): 'Lutescens' has brilliant silvery new foliage and white flowers, followed by red berries. (See p.12.) 'Chrysophylla' has yellow leaves throughout the summer. Upright; 16 × 10 ft (5 × 3 m); 26 × 20 ft (8 × 6 m).

S. aucuparia (rowan, mountain ash) has pinnate leaves, white flowers and red berries, which ripen at the beginning of August but are quickly stripped by birds. 'Fructu Luteo' has orange-yellow berries which are less rapidly eaten by birds. Upright; 20 × 13 ft (6 × 4 m); 30 × 20 ft (9 × 6 m).

S. cashmiriana bears pink flowers in May, followed by large white berries like glistening marbles, which last into the winter. Spreading; 13 × 13 ft (4 × 4 m); 20 × 23 ft (6 × 7 m).

S. commixta provides brilliant autumn colour, but does not flower or fruit well. Upright; 23 × 24 ft (7 × 4 m); 33 × 20 ft (10 × 6 m). 'Embley' is a form with glowing red autumn foliage.

Overleaf: *Prunus subhirtella* 'Pendula Rosea', a beautiful small umbrella-like tree, which has been grown in British gardens since the late nineteenth century

The violet willow, *Salix daphnoides*, is worth planting both for the colourful shoots and for the handsome yellow catkins, appearing in March before the leaves

S. folgneri is like a whitebeam with pendulous branches. The leaves turn russet in autumn on the upper surface, contrasting well with the vividly silvery undersides. Spreading; 16 × 10 ft (5 × 3 m); 30 × 20 ft (9 × 6 m).
S. glabrescens has small, shining white fruits, which continue long into the winter, and the leaves display fine red and yellow or orange-yellow colours in late October. Upright; 20 × 10 ft (6 × 3 m); 33 × 16 ft (10 × 5 m). It is usually offered under the name *S. hupehensis*, although the latter is distinguished by pinky berries and kite-shaped sea-green leaves. *S. forrestii* has larger white fruits and the foliage gives good autumn colour. Spreading; 10 × 6½ ft (3 × 2 m); 16 × 16 ft (5 × 5 m). Generally, birds do not touch the berries of white-fruited rowans until well into winter.
S. rehderiana 'Joseph Rock' has amber-yellow berries contrasting with the fiery crimson and purple of the autumn leaves and persisting for several weeks on the bare branches. Upright; 23 × 10 ft (7 × 3 m); 33 × 16 ft (10 × 5 m).

Overleaf: the gracefully weeping *Sophora japonica* 'Pendula' has rich green leaves divided into leaflets; it is excellent as a lawn tree or for making an arbour

S. scalaris has bold ladder-like leaves comprising numerous closely set leaflets and gives a long season of interest. The new leaves of dark crimson or bronze expand in April, then white flowers are carried in large dense heads in June, followed by the ripening red berries against the dark, glossy green leaves and finally the rich reds and purples of its autumn colour. Spreading; 13 × 16 ft (4 × 5 m); 20 × 26 ft (6 × 8 m). (See p.6 and p.57.)

S. vilmorinii has leaves composed of many small leaflets, which turn red and purple in autumn. The berries colour maroon or crimson in September and fade through pink to white. Spreading; 10 × 10 ft (3 × 3 m); 16 × 20 ft (5 × 6 m).

S. wardii is a whitebeam with ribbed leaves, grey downy when young, adopting russet colours in autumn. It is sometimes offered as *S. thibetica*, under the collector's number Kingdon Ward 21127. Upright; 13 × 6½ ft (4 × 2 m); 16 × 10 ft (5 × 3 m).

S. thibetica 'John Mitchell' (*S.* 'Mitchellii') has broad, nearly round, leaves, occasionally 8 in. (20 cm) long, bright silver beneath. Domed; 23 × 10 ft (7 × 3 m); 33 × 16 ft (10 × 5 m).

Staphylea Bladder nut

S. holocarpa has leaves consisting of three leaflets and carries panicles of pink flowers in spring on bare branches or with the bronze new foliage. The fruit is a pear-shaped bladder. Upright; 16 × 10 ft (5 × 3 m); 23 × 13 ft (7 × 4 m). (See p.63.)

Stuartia

S. pseudocamellia bears single, white, camellia-like flowers with a yellow boss of stamens in August. The bark is attractively flaky, while the leaves in autumn colour purplish, red or yellow. It is better on a moist lime-free soil. Upright; 16 × 10 ft (5 × 3 m); 30 × 16 ft (9 × 5 m).

Styrax

S. japonica (snowbell tree) has widespreading level branches, clothed in June with a mass of hanging bell-shaped flowers, white with yellow stamens. It prefers a moist lime-free soil in a sunny or semi-shaded position. Domed or conical; 10 × 6½ ft (3 × 2 m); 20 × 13 ft (6 × 4 m).

Thuja

T. koraiensis is evergreen and has leaves of matt yellow-green above, conspicuously silver beneath. The foliage has a strong fruity smell, especially when crushed. Upright; 10 × 6½ ft (3 × 2 m); 16 × 10 ft (5 × 3 m).

Tilia Lime, linden

T. mongolica (Mongolian lime) has prominent toothed leaves of glossy green, becoming yellow in autumn, and carries many fragrant small flowers in late July. Domed; 20 × 13 ft (6 × 4 m); 33 × 20 ft (10 × 6 m).

Trachycarpus

T. fortunei (Chusan palm) is an evergreen, which is hardy in southern and western Britain and probably in sheltered locations elsewhere, although young plants need winter protection. It slowly develops a tall trunk, covered with the fibrous bases of the leaves, and bears a cluster of enormous fan-shaped leaves, to nearly 4 ft (120 cm) across. Upright; 5 × 6½ ft (1.5 × 2 m); 10 × 6½ ft (3 × 2 m).

Tsuga Hemlock

T. heterophylla (western hemlock), an evergreen, is graceful as a young tree, with pendulous tips to the leading shoot and branches and dark green needles silvery beneath. It will thrive even in shady situations and on dry, acidic, sandy soils, although eventually growing too tall. Upright; 20 × 10 ft (6 × 3 m); 39 × 16 ft (12 × 5 m).

Overleaf: *Sorbus scalaris*, introduced from China in 1904, is a delightful small tree with a short trunk and broad crown

Opposite: After the showy flowers have faded, *Stuartia pseudocamellia* produces brilliant autumn colours from the leaves

Table: trees for specific situations and purposes

Category		Abies	Acer	Aesculus	Alnus	Aralia	Arbutus	Betula	Calocedrus	Carpinus	Catalpa	Cedrus	Cercidiphyllum	Cercis	Chamaecyparis	Cornus	Corylus	Cotoneaster	Crataegus	Cupressus	Decaisnea	Embothrium
features	ornamental bark		●				●													●		
	flowers	●				●	●				●			●		●	●	●	●	●	●	●
	fruits	●					●									●		●	●		●	
	coloured twigs		●		●																●	
	autumn tints		●					●		●			●			●			●			
foliage	variegated		●													●						
	gold/silver/grey/blue	●	●		●							●			●					●		
	purple		●																			
	coloured when young		●	●									●									
habit	fastigiate									●					●							●
	weeping				●			●				●										
	spreading/domed		●	●		●	●	●			●				●	●	●	●	●			
	upright/conical	●	●	●	●			●				●	●		●					●	●	
	deciduous		●	●	●	●		●		●	●		●	●		●	●		●		●	
	evergreen	●					●		●			●			●			●		●		●
situation	coastal		●				●											●	●	●		
	cold exposed		●		●			●	●									●	●	●		
	shade	●	●												●	●						
soil	wet/moist				●			●								●			●		●	●
	dry				●	●	●	●	●	●		●	●	●		●	●	●	●	●		
	chalk	●	●	●		●	●	●	●	●	●	●	●	●	●	●	●	●	●	●	●	

		Eucalyptus	Eucryphia	Euonymus	Fagus	Fraxinus	Genista	Ginkgo	Gleditsia	Halesia	Hydrangea	Ilex	Juniperus	Koelreuteria	Laburnum	Laurus	Ligustrum	Lindera	Magnolia	Mahonia	Malus	Metasequoia	Morus
features	ornamental bark	●																	●			●	
	flowers	●	●			●	●				●	●		●	●	●	●	●	●	●	●		
	fruits			●								●		●							●		●
	coloured twigs																						
	autumn tints			●	●			●	●									●			●	●	
foliage	variegated											●					●						
	gold/silver/grey/blue	●							●			●	●				●						
	purple				●																		
	coloured when young	●																					
habit	fastigiate				●			●					●										
	weeping			●	●							●	●										
	spreading/domed	●		●	●	●			●		●	●	●	●	●		●	●	●	●	●		●
	upright/conical	●	●		●	●	●	●		●				●		●	●		●		●	●	
	deciduous			●	●	●		●	●	●	●			●	●		●	●	●		●	●	●
	evergreen	●	●				●					●	●			●	●		●	●			
situation	coastal	●	●	●	●						●	●	●		●	●		●					
	cold exposed	●		●	●							●	●										
	shade			●	●							●	●										
soil	wet/moist			●	●					●		●						●	●			●	
	dry	●		●	●	●	●	●	●			●	●	●	●	●	●			●		●	
	chalk	●	●	●	●	●	●	●	●			●	●	●	●	●	●		●	●	●	●	●

Table: trees for specific situations and purposes

Category	Attribute	Nothofagus	Nyssa	Picea	Pinus	Prunus	Pyrus	Quercus	Rhus	Robinia	Salix	Sophora	Sorbus	Staphylea	Stuartia	Styrax	Tilia	Thuja	Trachycarpus	Tsuga
features	ornamental bark				•	•						•			•				•	
	flowers			•	•	•	•			•	•		•	•	•	•	•			
	fruits			•	•															
	coloured twigs										•									
	autumn tints	•	•			•		•	•				•		•					
foliage	variegated																			
	gold/silver/grey/blue			•	•		•			•	•		•					•		•
	purple												•							
	coloured when young	•				•	•			•										
habit	fastigiate					•												•		
	weeping					•	•				•	•								•
	spreading/domed		•			•	•	•	•	•	•	•	•	•		•	•			
	upright/conical	•	•	•	•	•				•	•		•	•	•	•		•	•	•
	deciduous	•	•			•	•	•	•	•	•	•	•	•	•	•	•			
	evergreen			•	•													•	•	•
situation	coastal			•	•						•		•							
	cold exposed	•		•	•						•		•					•		•
	shade																	•		•
soil	wet/moist	•	•	•	•		•				•		•		•	•		•		•
	dry			•	•	•	•	•		•		•	•					•	•	•
	chalk			•	•	•	•	•	•	•	•	•	•	•		•		•	•	•

SOME SHRUBS FOR TRAINING AS TREES

(See also the Wisley handbook, *Shrubs for small gardens*.)
Amelanchier lamarckii
Berberis francisci–ferdinandii, B. jamesiana, B. valdiviana
Buddleja alternifolia, B. colvilei, B. davidii
Camellia × *williamsii*
Corylopsis veitchiana
Cotinus coggygria
Cytisus battandieri
Dipelta floribunda
Elaeagnus pungens
Exochorda giraldii
Hippophae rhamnoides
Lonicera maackii
Mespilus germanica
Parrotia persica
Philadelphus 'Virginal'
Photinia (Stranvaesia) davidiana
Stachyurus chinensis
Syringa yunnanensis

The unusual bladder nut, *Staphylea holocarpa*, may be grown as a tree or large shrub

The Katsura tree, *Cercidiphyllum japonicum*, has small heart-shaped leaves similar to those of the Judas tree, which colour dramatically in autumn